A TIME *of* WAR

The Inevitable Conflict Between the Church of Today and the Church of Tomorrow

STUDY GUIDE

Published by AVAIL

Cover design by: Joe De Leon
Photography by: Andrew van Tilborgh

ISBN: 978-1-954089-44-0 1 2 3 4 5 6 7 8 9 10

Printed in the United States of America

STUDY GUIDE

A TIME *of* WAR

The Inevitable Conflict Between the Church of Today and the Church of Tomorrow

MARTIJN VAN TILBORGH

CONTENTS

CHAPTER ONE

THE UNAVOIDABLE CONFLICT: WHY CHANGE HAS TO HAPPEN

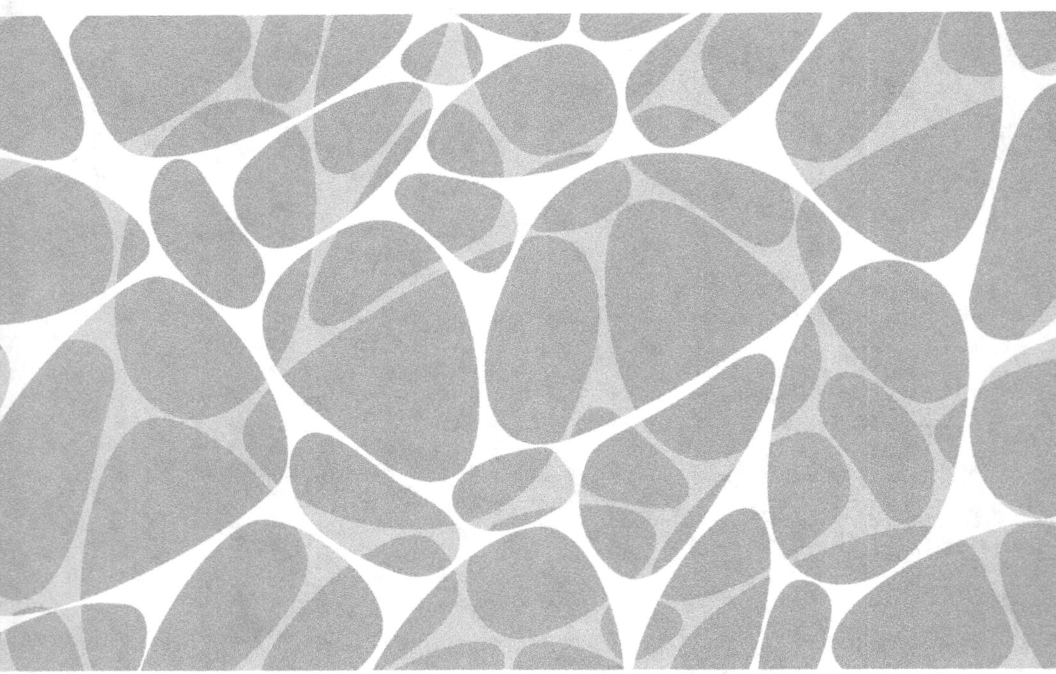

Innovation happens at the edge of chaos. It happens where the developed land stops, and undeveloped land—chaos—starts. It only happens where chaos is cultivated into new opportunities that will advance the kingdom into places it couldn't get before.

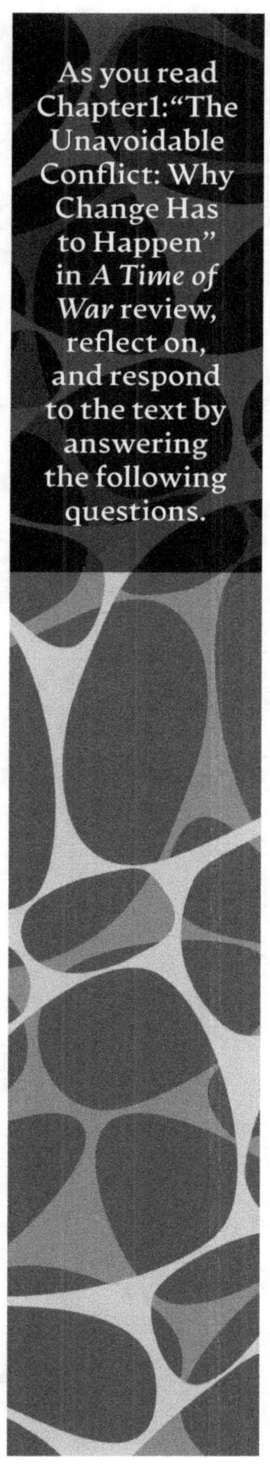

REVIEW, REFLECT, AND RESPOND:

How can we compare the differences between Saul and David to the conflict and tension we are currently seeing within the church?

What was different about David's approach that allowed for his endeavors to be successful?

Why do we, as leaders, find it so difficult to elevate out of the "weeds" and minutia to gain a kingdom perspective so that we can see further ahead?

What is the difference between innovation and adaptation?

How can optimization "trick" us into thinking we are innovating?

But many of the older priests and Levites and family heads, who had seen the former temple, wept aloud when they saw the foundation of this temple being laid, while many others shouted for joy. —Ezra 3:12 (NIV)

Consider the Scripture above and answer the following questions:

Why do you think it is difficult for those from the "old order" to celebrate with the success of the new generation?

What can believers from all generations do to create a forward-facing focus?

Share another example from God's Word in which there was conflict and tension between old and new.

Have you ever found yourself digging in the weeds and neglecting to soar high for that bird's eye view? How did you let go and take off?

Share a time when you were adaptive, not innovative, or a time when you were optimizing an already existing program or idea.

CHAPTER TWO

SEEING THINGS CLEARLY: GETTING A TRUE PERSPECTIVE

We need to open ourselves to alternative realities beyond our current one so that our perception of the world around us can be aligned with "truth" and we lead more effectively.

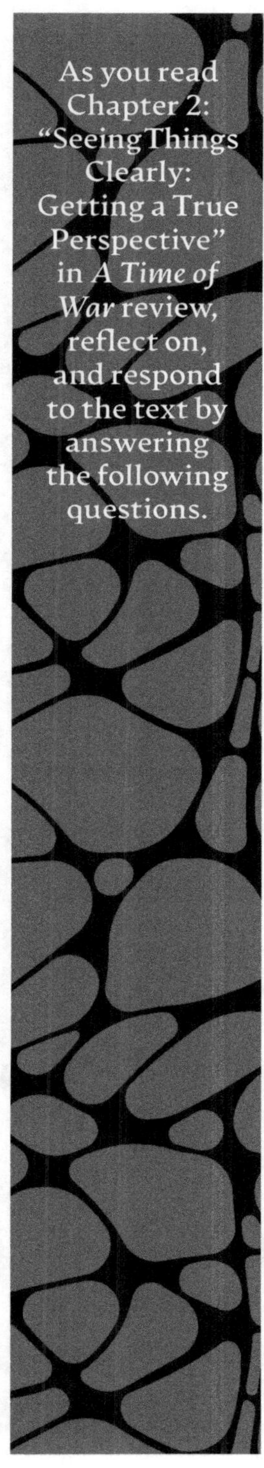

REVIEW, REFLECT, AND RESPOND:

Martijn shared some ways that our perception can be conditioned. What other realities tend to shape our perceptions?

Do you think it's possible to self-identify the realities that may taint our perception? How could those be addressed in an effort to align with "truth"?

Consider the younger generation under Moses who were forced to become shepherds for forty years. How do you think that affected their perception?

Although they knew the "truth" of the promised land, they experienced a different reality. How might that have influenced the way they raised up the generation beneath them?

Do you think the modern-day church has become one of those shepherds? Why or why not?

The Lord has torn the kingdom of Israel from you today, and has given it to a neighbor of yours, who is better than you. —1 Samuel 15:27 (NKJV)

Consider the Scripture above and answer the following questions:

What are the dangers of the church following the standards set by the culture?

What can we learn from Saul, that although he was an excellent leader by human standards, he wasn't who or what (a king) God intended for His people?

Did Saul have any choices other than the path he was on once he realized David's anointing?

As a "Jonathan," what are some ways that you feel pulled in multiple directions?

How can we grow ourselves in confidence to commit to the future versus cling to the past and unhealthy loyalties?

What can you do to ensure that your own Jonathans have the freedom to follow God's destiny?

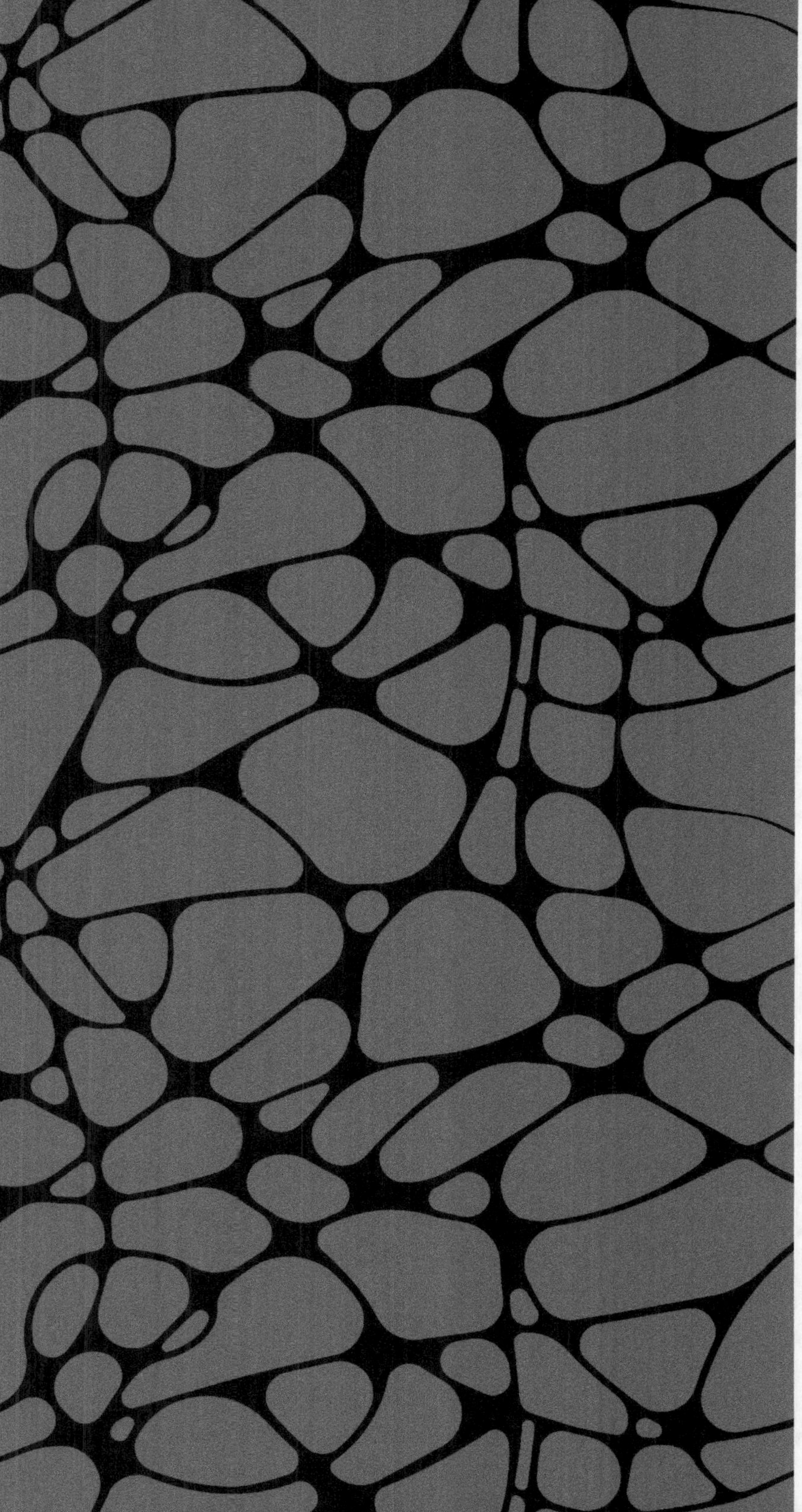

CHAPTER THREE

JUDGES, PRIESTS, PROPHETS, AND KINGS: THE EVOLUTION OF GODLY LEADERSHIP

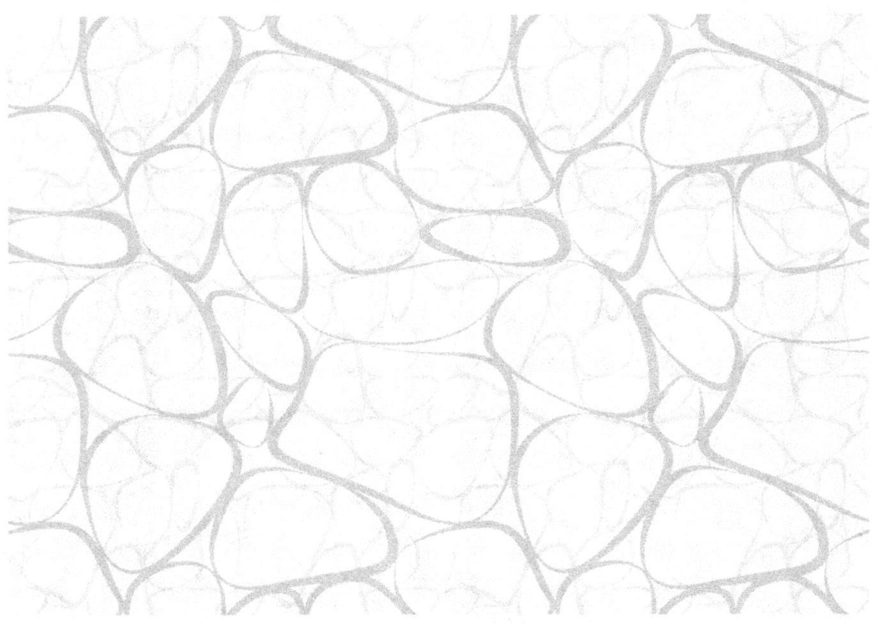

A shift is required for each generation to manifest something new in its time. That shift requires it to detach itself from the past to expand God's kingdom in the future.

As you read Chapter 3: "Judges, Priests, Prophets, and Kings: The Evolution of Godly Leadership" in *A Time of War* review, reflect on, and respond to the text by answering the following questions.

REVIEW, REFLECT, AND RESPOND:

What is the problem with looking to the past for guidance on current realities? Is there a benefit? Why or why not?

What were the various leadership models that Saul had to glean from? How was David able to pull away from that history?

Consider the great "judges" throughout the history of Christendom—those who facilitated great moves of God. How does their temporary nature help and hinder the kingdom at large?

What are the benefits of the Eli "priest" model of ministry? What are the drawbacks?

As a prophet, Samuel knew he was called to minister in more than one place. What sort of mental shift did those "on his staff" need to also make? How have you required those you lead to shift with you?

The Lord gave David victory wherever he went.

—Chronicles 18:6 (NIV)

Consider the Scripture above and answer the following questions:

What do you find to be the most encouraging aspect of this Scripture?

How should we seek to find this kind of favor with God?

Do you know WHO you are, WHAT you are supposed to be doing, and WHERE you should be doing it?

What model of leadership do you most identify with? How is that evident in your own history?

What can we glean from the knowledge that Saul neglected God's presence during his tenure as king?

CHAPTER FOUR

A FAITH EARTHQUAKE: WHEN EVERYTHING CHANGES

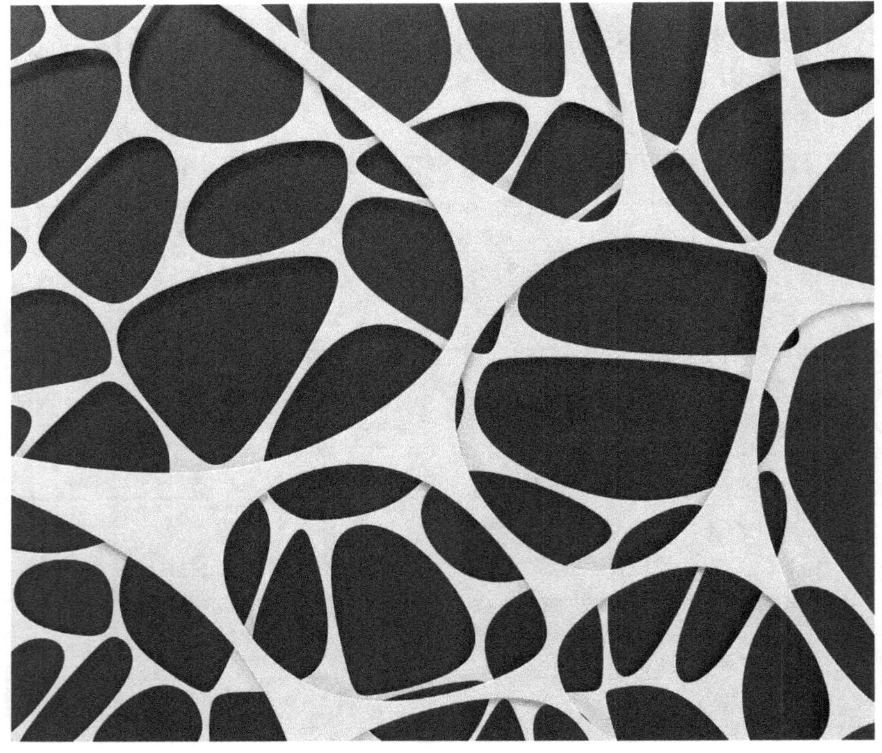

We can't bring kingdom culture to the church. We need to bring our churches to kingdom culture.

As you read Chapter 4: "A Faith Earthquake: When Everything Changes" in *A Time of War* review, reflect on, and respond to the text by answering the following questions.

REVIEW, REFLECT, AND RESPOND:

Describe the discrepancy between prophetic revelation and apostolic manifestation. How does this differentiation impact those who are "stuck" in revelation?

As you receive revelation about the future of God's kingdom on earth, how can you prepare to move?

Consider the actions of Elisha when he not only released the next generation, but also went with them. What are the implications of this?

What did Elisha gain by going with the next generation? What did they gain by honoring him and his presence?

What are the differences between kingdom culture and church culture?

But seek the kingdom of God, and all these things shall be added to you.

—Luke 12:31 (NKJV)

Consider the Scripture above and answer the following questions:

God's Word refers to the kingdom He wants to establish on the earth dozens of times. How does this emphasis impact how we present the Gospel?

How can we share the importance of a "kingdom-first" mentality?

What are some ways that a shift can be made from church culture to kingdom culture?

Have you ever found yourself in a place like Martijn did, doing God's work only to realize that He never asked you to do that thing to begin with? Did you continue the work or let go? How did that decision impact your trajectory?

Share a story from your past in which you made a mindset change and shifted toward God's calling for your life.

What are some areas that you can identify the need for a shift in your mindset?

CHAPTER FIVE

SETTLING FOR SAUL: WHEN A GODLY DESIRE IS DISTORTED

God created us in His image. If He is a King and we are created in His image, then He effectively created us to operate like kings in His kingdom. Because of the genesis of God's kingdom and what His intended purpose was with creation, I believe He deposited a desire, a drive, in every human being to rule and reign.

As you read Chapter 5: "Settling for Saul: When a Godly Desire is Distorted" in *A Time of War* review, reflect on, and respond to the text by answering the following questions.

REVIEW, REFLECT, AND RESPOND:

Martijn discusses the Israelites "weary hearts" and "wrong conclusions." Why were their hearts weary?

What lead to their wrong conclusions?

What sort of king did God have in mind for the Israelites?

As a ruler over God's domain, how are we active kings in His kingdom?

Since all humans have the desire for kingship, why is a personal relationship with God so critical to fulfilling His destiny?

...hope deferred makes the heart sick...

—Proverbs 13:12 (NKJV)

Consider the Scripture above and answer the following questions:

How did the discrepancy between their promises and their reality cause the Israelites to demand a king?

How can a person find confident hope when their destiny is unfulfilled with no victory in sight?

What are some ways that you can encourage others to take their position as kings in God's kingdom?

In God's government, kings, priests, and prophets are all necessary components. How do you see that practically applied to the church today?

____

____

____

____

____

____

____

As the church makes this shift into kingdom mindsets, what do we have to give up? What are we willing to leave behind?

____

____

____

____

____

____

____

How will we know when it's time to move?

____

____

____

____

____

____

____

CHAPTER SIX

NO MORE SECOND BEST: CREATORS, NOT COPYCATS

Once saved, we have access to that kingdom. Not doing so is disrespectful to the One who paid the price to get it for us. And even if we don't want it for ourselves, the world around us needs it.

As you read Chapter 6: "No More Second Best: Creators, Not Copycats" in *A Time of War* review, reflect on, and respond to the text by answering the following questions.

REVIEW, REFLECT, AND RESPOND:

Why does Martijn feel that we undervalue the kingdom of God by "merely" going to heaven?

How has the church fallen into second place, where we are no longer thought leaders in culture?

Consider the spheres of influence that create culture. How can we increase the kingdom influence in those areas?

Continue with Martijn's list of a "million little things" that create culture by naming more here. How does this translate to expanding kingdom culture in any or all of these areas?

Why would a "place" such as Ramah or Shiloh dampen or dispel the influence of a king?

Then the Lord appeared to Solomon by night, and said to him: 'I have heard your prayer, and have chosen this place for Myself as a house of sacrifice.' —2 Chronicles 7:12 (NKJV)

Consider the Scripture above and answer the following questions:

What can we learn from the wisdom of Solomon regarding his acknowledgement of inadequacy?

Solomon still built the temple to honor God. How does that translate to your giftings or area of cultural influence?

Describe a time that God honored or blessed your sacrifices and efforts in spite of your shortcomings.

When Martijn "saw" the kingdom of God while the televangelist was preaching, he immediately had a faith crisis? What sort of similar experience have you had?

How can we promote critical thinking skills in the church today?

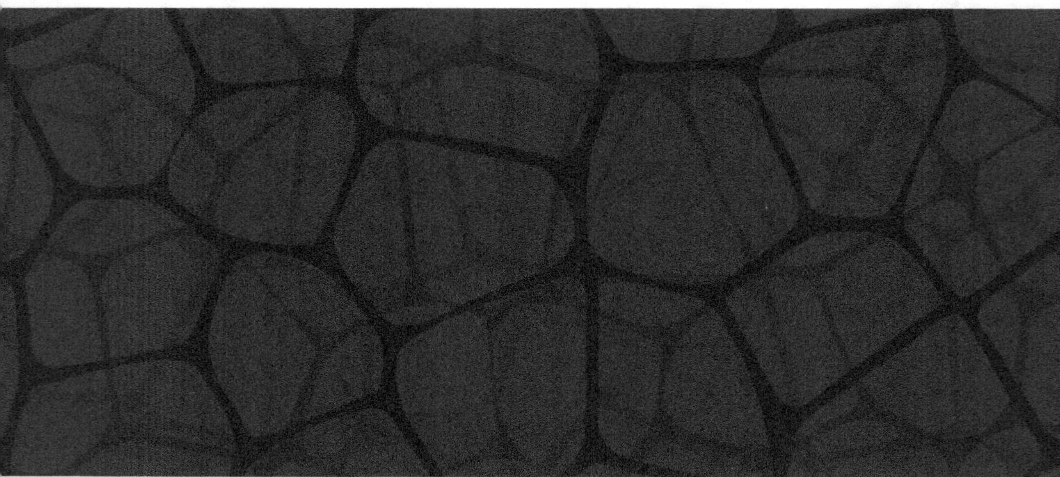

CHAPTER SEVEN

GOD'S KINGDOM DICTIONARY: LEARNING TO SPEAK HIS LANGUAGE

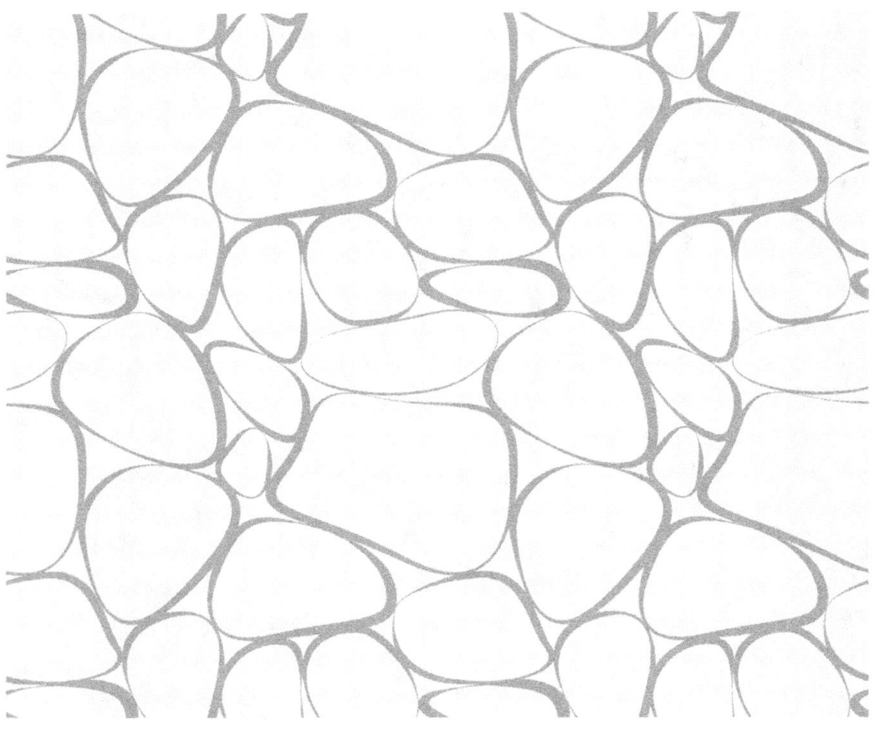

Never settle when it comes to revelation. There is always something more to understand. There is always a higher way.

As you read Chapter 7: “God'sKingdom Dictionary: Learning to Speak His Language” in *A Time of War* review, reflect on, and respond to the text by answering the following questions.

REVIEW, REFLECT, AND RESPOND:

What are some “big-picture” impact areas of culture that are important to invade with kingdom culture?

What are some examples of words that mean different things in different countries (such as costume)?

Share any scriptural words that have deviated from their original meanings in the church (such as *ekklesia*). How has that affected the presentation of God's kingdom?

What does the term "progressive revelation" mean? Do you think there is a structure or timeline associated with this dynamic or is it based on a person's openness to new insight?

How would you describe the concept of the dying seed?

'The glory of this latter temple shall be greater than the former,' says the Lord of hosts. 'And in this place I will give peace,' says the Lord of hosts. —Haggai 2:9 (NKJV)

Consider the Scripture above and answer the following questions:

Why is it so difficult for many people to let go of the former things when God is clear in His promise that the new things are greater?

____

____

____

____

____

____

What do we stand to gain by trusting God's promise on this?

____

____

____

____

____

____

How is this Scripture relevant to today's cultural context?

____

____

____

____

____

Describe a time in which God used YOU as the window of blessing.

How can you prepare your heart and mind for continuous revelation? Is it possible to endlessly progress in understanding?

As we consider the kingdom context within our economy, how do we share this message with others?

CHAPTER EIGHT

A NEW KIND OF KINGDOM: A FAMILY, NOT AN INSTITUTION

As God's nation, we are not a country. We are not defined by lines on a map or by the passport we carry. A nation is connected by blood. A nation is family.

REVIEW, REFLECT, AND RESPOND:

As you read Chapter 8: "A New Kind of Kingdom: A Family, Not an Institution" in *A Time of War* review, reflect on, and respond to the text by answering the following questions.

How is God's kingdom different from any kingdom on earth?

As we consider our role in administrating God's kingdom, how can that change our perspective on everyday interactions with those "outside" the kingdom (unbelievers)?

Think of your own family business or one you know of. What can we understand about God's operational desires through this structure?

What does God mean by creating a nation? Why does He want to create a nation like this?

Consider Martijn's interpretation of family in God's kingdom. How does that affect the way we operate as family members globally?

For I do not seek yours, but you. For the children ought not to lay up for the parents, but the parents for the children. —2 Corinthians 12:14 (NKJV)

Consider the Scripture above and answer the following questions:

This desire is in direct opposition to the world's kingdoms. How do we model this in an attractive way?

This kingdom does not take away, but adds to its citizens. What can we do to add to the kingdom ourselves?

In thinking about the side effects of a worldly kingdom as listed by Samuel, what are some situations you've found yourself in that you felt your "service" was taken advantage of?

Describe the tension of the "organizational church" and the "organic family of God" as you see it.

Knowing that our kingship is inherited, what are you doing to ensure that the next generation of leaders is aware of this and embraces their place in God's kingdom family?

CHAPTER NINE

THE KEY TO KINGDOM GROWTH: TEARING DOWN THE WALLS

Kingdom expansion doesn't happen through institution and/or control. It happens through empowering people to live their dreams.

As you read Chapter 9: "The Key to Kingdom Growth: Tearing Down the Walls" in *A Time of War* review, reflect on, and respond to the text by answering the following questions.

REVIEW, REFLECT, AND RESPOND:

Recall the man traveling to build a wall around Jerusalem. Why do you think the angel stopped him from continuing to his task?

Have you ever developed your talent or skill only for it to become "irrelevant"? How did you respond?

Thinking about eliminating measuring tools as progress, how does that change a ministry's paradigm?

Describe Martijn's loose connections between communism and traditional church leadership. What are some ways that we can recognize and set "alarm bells" when a ministry may be too institutionalized?

Remember the walls and canals in the Netherlands—why would a city planner repeatedly place predefined limitations on the future? What is the correction?

But this is what was spoken by the prophet Joel: "And it shall come to pass in the last days, says God, That I will pour out of My Spirit on all flesh; Your sons and your daughters shall prophesy, Your young men shall see visions, Your old men shall dream dreams." —Acts 2:16-17 (NKJV)

Consider the Scripture above and answer the following questions:

When God pours His Spirit, how does that help manifest His kingdom?

Why would a kingdom culture be more conducive to an outpouring of God's Spirit than "church" culture?

Once God's people receive their dreams and visions, what is the best way to allow the growth of those dreams and visions?

If kingdom expansion comes through empowerment, not control, how can church leaders press to promote that environment?

How do we "break down walls" without offending those who have not opened up to kingdom culture (yet)?

What are the benefits of each citizen of the kingdom living his or her dream?

CHAPTER TEN

A NEW HORIZON: LOOKING AT CHURCH DIFFERENTLY

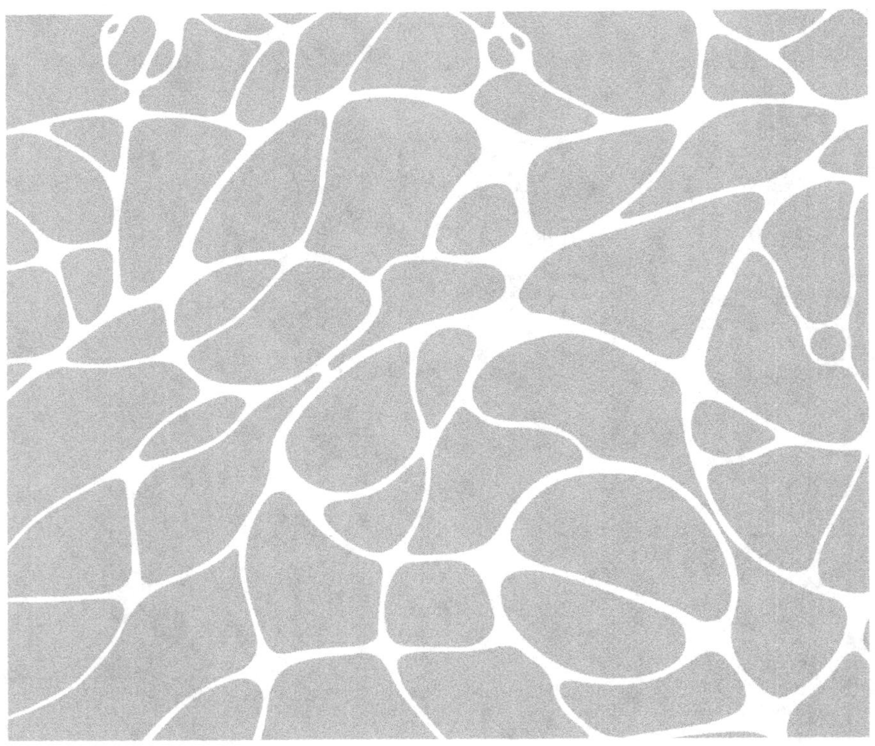

Trade happens in every sphere and segment of society. By allowing it to become the infrastructure and distribution model for the kingdom, we will be able to reach every corner of our communities organically.

As you read Chapter 10: "A New Horizon: Looking at Church Differently" in *A Time of War* review, reflect on, and respond to the text by answering the following questions.

REVIEW, REFLECT, AND RESPOND:

What was significant about the inside-out vision of "pushing people out instead of pulling people in"?

____

____

____

____

____

____

____

____

____

____

How does this relate to the shift we are experiencing from the "church model" to the "kingdom model"?

____

____

____

____

____

____

____

____

____

____

____

How have we as church leaders limited the "shape of water"?

Where does Martijn see an opportunity for kingdom expansion as we encourage others to become "liquid leaders"?

Jesus told them another parable: "The kingdom of heaven is like a man who sowed good seed in his field. But while everyone was sleeping, his enemy came and sowed weeds among the wheat, and went away. When the wheat sprouted and formed heads, then the weeds also appeared. The owner's servants came to him and said, 'Sir, didn't you sow good seed in your field? Where then did the weeds come from?' 'An enemy did this,' he replied. The servants asked him, 'Do you want us to go and pull them up?' 'No,' he answered, 'because while you are pulling the weeds, you may uproot the wheat with them. Let both grow together until the harvest.'" —Matthew 13:24-30 (NKJV)

Consider the Scripture above and answer the following questions:

What are the dangers of separating ourselves from the tares of this world?

____

____

____

____

____

What does Paul's ministry route have to do with this story? How can we recognize and equip Christians to be "liquid leaders" amongst the tares?

____

____

____

____

____

____

____

How can Facebook be a sort of model to consider as a picture of God's kingdom?

How can church leaders encourage people to be authentic and seek their unique calling and identity?

Consider the possibilities when we utilize trade to share the gospel and kingdom of God. Jot down any specific ideas that come to your mind here.

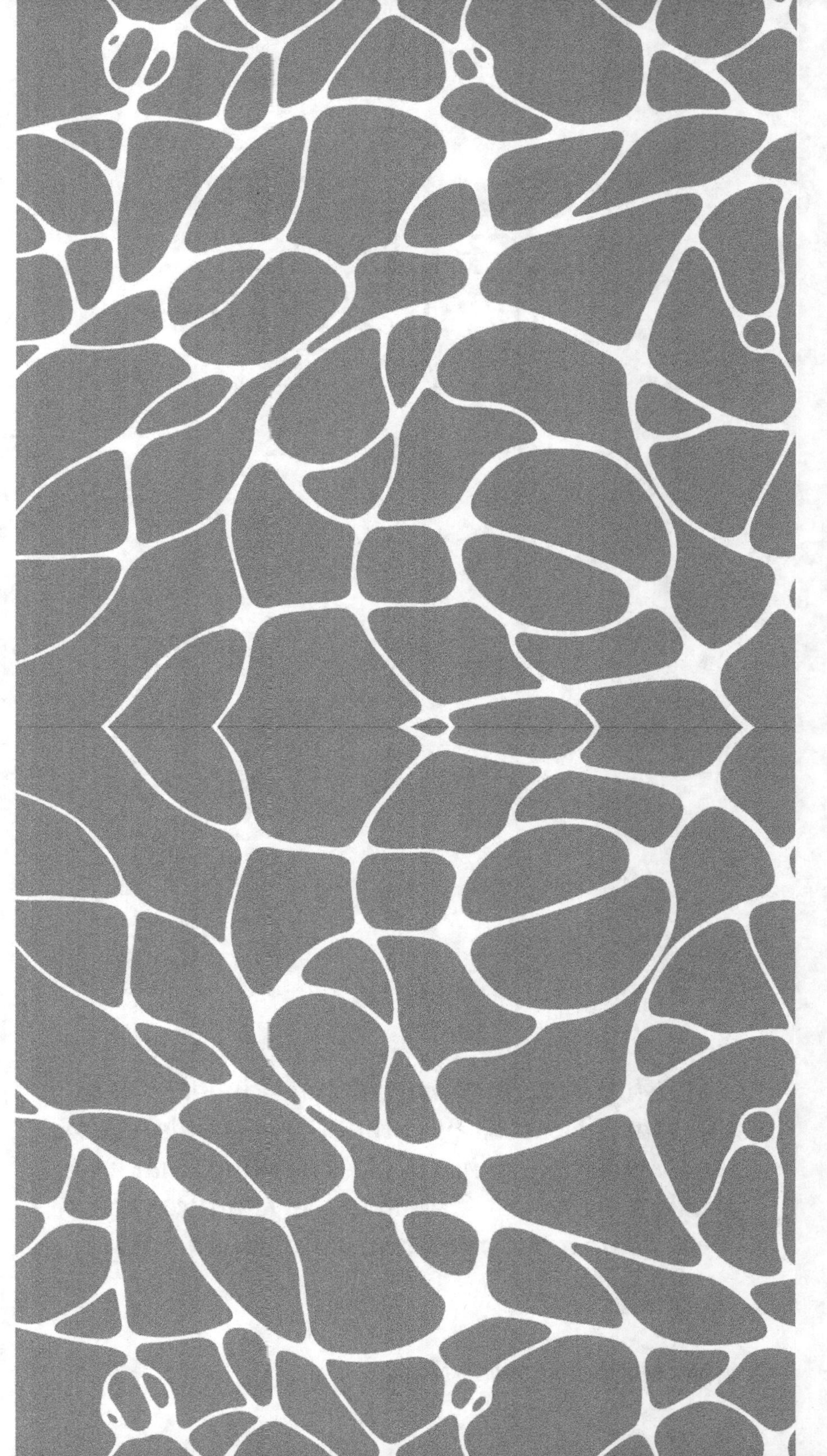

CHAPTER ELEVEN

SACRIFICE OVER EXCELLENCE: THE HEART OF CHANGE

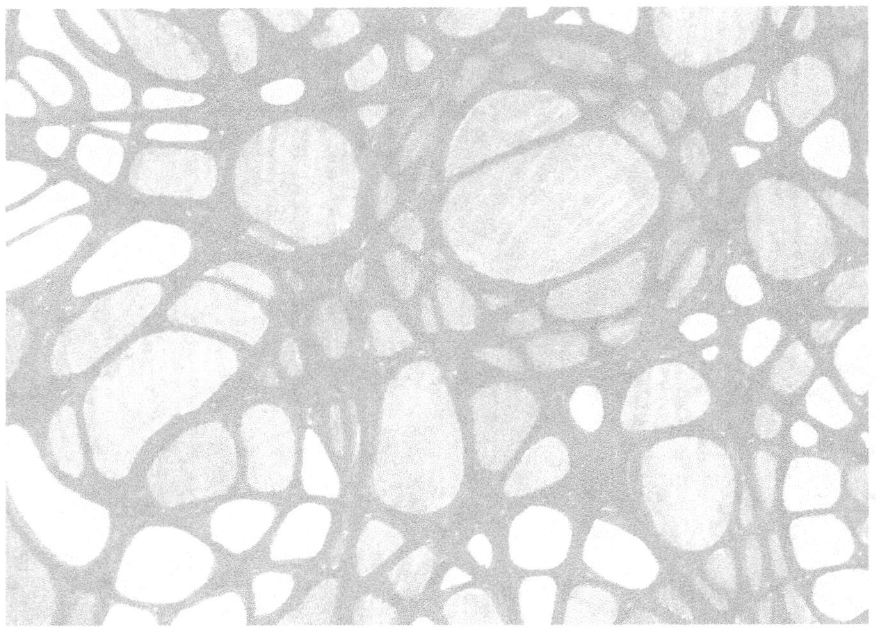

The shift between "church" and "kingdom" is a shift that will cost us everything. It demands that we leave behind the things of old. The things that have worked in the past. Trying to shortcut the process by doing it any other way will cost us greatly.

As you read Chapter 11: "Sacrifice over Excellence: The Heart of Change" in *A Time of War* review, reflect on, and respond to the text by answering the following questions.

REVIEW, REFLECT, AND RESPOND:

Why must the church and marketplace come together in "Jerusalem" to be able to coexist?

Have you ever attempted to accomplish something "new" with an "old" method? What would you redo if you had the chance?

Why did David decide to "store" the ark and take a break to figure out his next move?

What did David do differently the second time he tried to move the ark? Why do you think these changes were important to his success?

Why does sacrifice top the list of what's necessary to bring God's kingdom?

And so it was, when those bearing the ark of the Lord had gone six paces, that he sacrificed oxen and fatted sheep. Then David danced before the Lord with all his might. —2 Samuel 6:13-14 (NKJV)

Consider the Scripture above and answer the following questions:

Think about the logistics it took in time, resources, and energy to make this journey. What is a comparable sacrifice in today's terms?

____

____

____

____

____

Why do you think David made this shift in moving forward with the ark?

____

____

____

____

____

What does this speak to the value God places on sacrifice?

____

____

____

____

____

Recall a time that you chose the wrong person to lead a project or venture. What was the result? Were you able to recover?

Have you ever been ANGRY and AFRAID with the results of your choices while you thought you were doing the right thing? How did you emerge from that situation?

What does David's willingness to "do whatever it took" to successfully move the ark (sacrifices, wearing an ephod, dancing like crazy) mean for us as church leaders today?

CHAPTER TWELVE

TRAINING FOR REIGNING: THE HARD PATH TO KINGSHIP

Wrong behavior is never justified because someone is anointed.

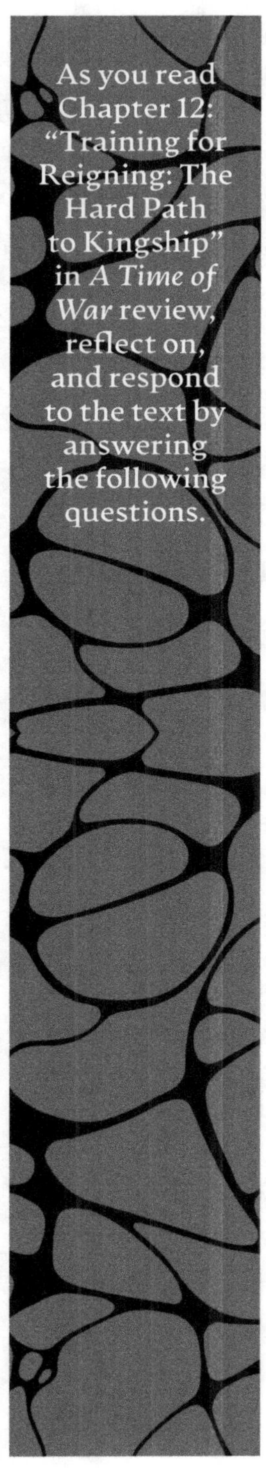

REVIEW, REFLECT, AND RESPOND:

Why would Saul take away everyone else's weapons? What was the consequence of that decision?

When Saul threatened the people to join him in battle, what sort of culture was he creating by making his consequential demands?

Saul's kingship wasn't marked for destruction until he chose to disobey Samuel and do what the people wanted. What does this indicate for church leaders as we seek God's perfect timing?

David's rejection of the "old" armor and his embrace of his "new" unique gifting is an important key for us to grasp. Why?

As David was running from Saul, the numbers in his "misfit" group began to grow. What is the significance of that time period and his accumulation of followers?

> *Then those who feared the Lord spoke to one another, And the Lord listened and heard them; So a book of remembrance was written before Him For those who fear the Lord And who meditate on His name.*
>
> *—Malachi 3:16 (NKJV)*

Consider the Scripture above and answer the following questions:

As you reflect on the ideas presented in this book, who are some people you can connect with on this journey?

____

____

____

____

____

What are your plans for documenting your journey as you shift into a kingdom culture?

____

____

____

____

____

What are some questions you have as you begin this journey?

____

____

____

____

____

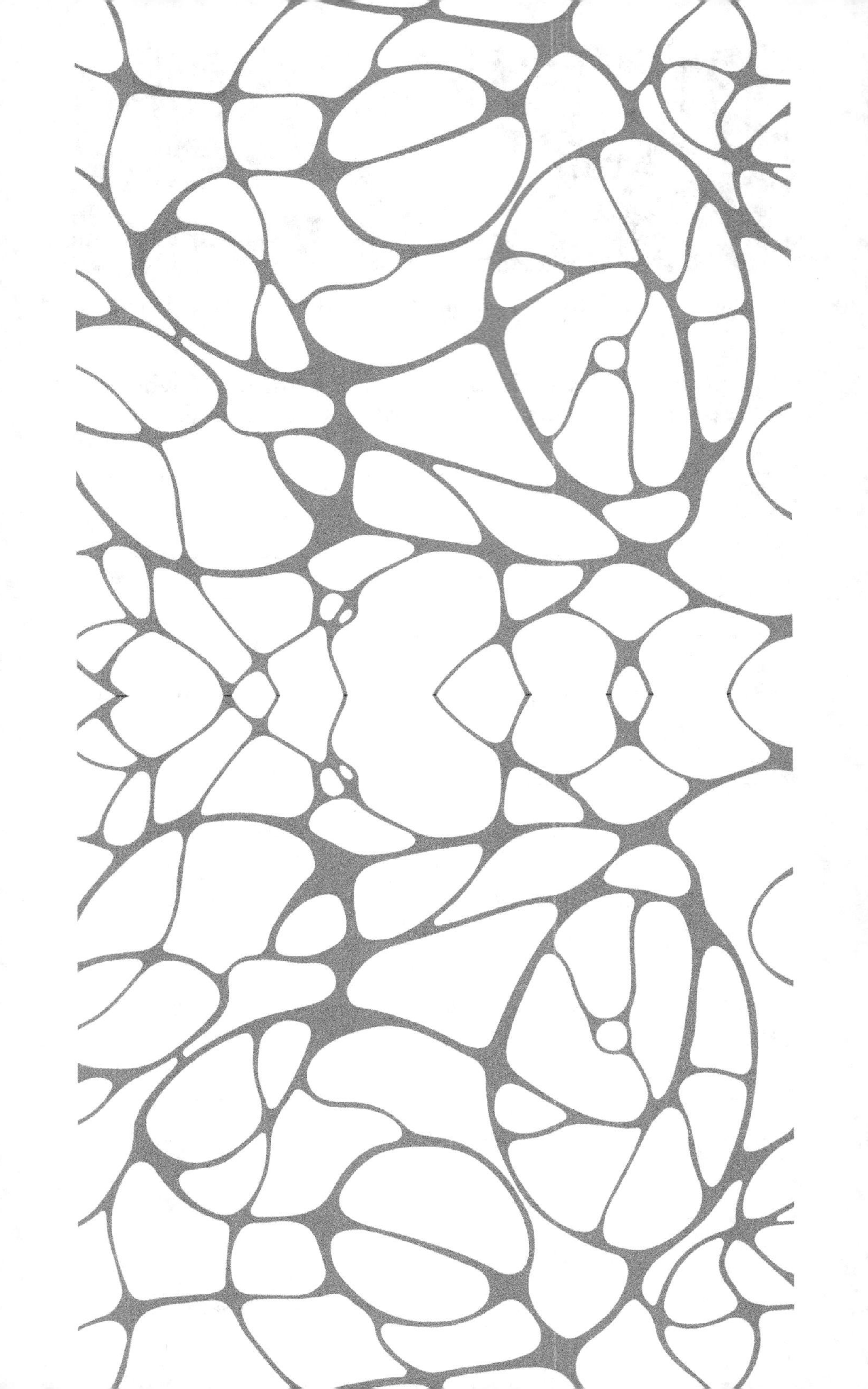

What was the top differentiating factor between Saul and David?

What do you believe to be the most critical tension points between the house of David and the house of Saul?

What can you do from your position to encourage the shift from church culture to kingdom culture?

www.ingramcontent.com/pod-product-compliance
Lightning Source LLC
LaVergne TN
LVHW020049110826
845155LV00029B/700

* 9 7 8 1 9 5 4 0 8 9 4 4 0 *